HEALING IS

A WORKBOOK FOR THE

REINVISIONED YOU

Curated by

Konniesha Moulton, LMFT & Felicia Fdyfil-Horne, LCSW

AuthorHouse™
1663 Liberty Drive
Bloomington, IN 47403
www.authorhouse.com
Phone: 833-262-8899

This book is printed on acid-free paper.

ISBN: 978-1-6655-2829-0 (sc)
ISBN: 978-1-6655-2828-3 (e)

Print information available on the last page.

Published by AuthorHouse 06/23/2021

authorHOUSE®

THE JOURNEY

Message from the Curators,

Thank you for taking the time out to focus on you. This was a project of love because we know first-hand the importance of healing. Utilize this book as a tool in your arsenal, whether you are beginning your journey to healing or in the thick of the work. Use it along with other tools, such as therapy or social groups. Work through it more than once, until it feels that you are at the place you deserve to be, the reinvisioned you.

With Sincere Gratitude,

Konniesha and Felicia

HEALING IS....

5 REASONS WHY

YOU SHOULD USE THIS WORKBOOK

1. Research has proven that shifting your thoughts and internal scripts to a more positive and self-affirming space can drastically enhance your daily functioning.

2. Most of our thoughts are unconscious, by using this workbook and making them conscious you can decrease the power they have over your emotions and behaviors.

3. This workbook is a user-friendly self-guided tool for self-development. Please go at your own pace and allow yourself to intentionally sit through the process.

4. This process will take commitment in order to unlock your potential. This will be a guidebook to remind you of who you were, who you are, and who you are becoming.

5. Healing is not linear; it is an ongoing process. Embrace the journey.

HEALING IS....

RADICAL GRATITUDE

According to the Oxford Dictionary, gratitude is the quality of being thankful; readiness to show appreciation for and to return kindness. "Radical gratitude" is taking it up a notch. It is ensuring that we hold on to what is good in life, no matter who we are or our past experiences. It is looking at the small things and appreciating them. It is noticing the same blue bird outside the window, the same time every year. It is enjoying the smells of Sunday dinner being cooked. It is being thankful for it all, even in-the-midst of the crazy thing we call life.

COMMITTING TO IT EVERYDAY

MORNING

Date:_____

Today I look forward to

_____

_____

_____

Today I am going to pay particular attention to

_____

_____

_____

EVENING

My favorite part of today was

_____

_____

COMMITTING TO IT EVERYDAY

MORNING

Date:_____

Today I look forward to

_____

_____

_____

Today I am going to pay particular attention to

_____

_____

_____

EVENING

My favorite part of today was

_____

_____

COMMITTING TO IT EVERYDAY

MORNING

Date:_____

Today I look forward to

_____

_____

_____

Today I am going to pay particular attention to

_____

_____

_____

EVENING

My favorite part of today was

_____

_____

RADICAL GRATITUDE IS....

COMMITTING TO IT EVERYDAY

MORNING

Date:_____

Today I look forward to

_____

_____

_____

Today I am going to pay particular attention to

_____

_____

_____

EVENING

My favorite part of today was

_____

_____

HEALING IS....

SELF COMPASSION

Currently, "Self-Care" has gained popularity in recent years, showing up in ad campaigns and movies. Depictions of bubbles baths, outings with friends, taking personal and quiet time, reading or vacationing have all shown us what the term "Self-Care" is supposed to look like. Yet "Self-Care" is only a part of the healing process. True healing begins once we dig deeper with loving ourselves by offering ourselves compassion. Especially when life is giving you lemons and there is no sugar to make lemonade.

PRACTICING NO: Not everything deserves a yes, sometimes we offer ourselves as sacrificial lambs for the sake of our career, our marriage, our family, and the list goes on. Sometimes we MUST give ourselves permission to say NO... Let us practice:

One thing that I always say YES to, but should sometimes (_maybe always_) say NO to

_____

_____

_____

One thing that I say NO to myself but should say YES to

_____

_____

_____

I pledge to say NO and choose me by

_____

_____

_____

GIVING YOURSELF GRACE: It is the moments where you messed up, maybe even more than once or twice. It is forgiving yourself, even when the world won't forgive you (funny enough the world is not even paying attention). It is not that you should never correct your wrongs, or continually make excuses for those wrongs. It is acknowledging that we all are flawed, because that is what being human is all about.

I forgive myself for

_____

_____

_____

I forgive myself for

_____

_____

_____

I forgive myself for

_____

_____

_____

GIVING YOURSELF GRACE:

Today I gave myself grace when _____

- -

Yesterday I gave myself grace for_____

- -

Tomorrow I will give myself grace when _____

- -

Today I gave myself grace when _____

- -

Yesterday I gave myself grace for_____

- -

Tomorrow I will give myself grace when _____

- -

PRAISING YOURSELF: You ever heard the phrase often used for children, "catch them being good"? It is about looking for the moments that your children are doing the things you want them to, instead of focusing on the times they are doing all the things that make you scream. Well as adults, it is important to do the same thing. We often focus on times we missed the mark and the times when we weren't our A+ selves. We never pat ourselves on the back for the times when we got it right, the times when you persevered after missing the mark. Create a daily habit where you give yourself some "SHINE", KUDOS, YOU GO (insert name here), YOU DID THAT!!!! Catch yourself being the awesome you, that you are.

One thing I am proud of myself for is

_____

_____

_____

I did (FILL IN) well today

_____

_____

- -

SAYING YES TO OURSELVES

Have you said yes to yourself? Have you chosen yourself for the moment, for the day, for the week?

1. What do you like to do?

_____

_____

_____

2. When was the last time you did it?

_____

_____

_____

3. When was the last time you said yes to someone else, but no to yourself?

_____

_____

_____

If you were able to answer question three quickly, but not question
2, commit to saying yes to yourself right now. If not, still commit
to saying yes to yourself, as often as you can today.

HEALING IS....

ATTUNEMENT

What is attunement you may ask? Attunement is the action of zooming into ourselves. Have you ever taken a picture and zoomed in to how you look and noticed every minute detail, the size of your pores, the way your feet are pointed? While it is similar, it is different as we are not looking to be critical. We are instead tuning into our emotional, physical, and mental well-being. We use it as a key, to see what we may need in that moment. This can be done at any time, whether it is in the middle of rush hour or laying on a beach. In order to know what we need, to take care of ourselves in that moment, we need to zoom in.

<u>BODY SCAN: Zooming into your body. (This works best when you practice daily or several times a day).</u>

Getting Started:

1. Get comfortable. You can do this while sitting down or laying down, do what feels most comfortable for you.

2. Breathe. As you breath in through your nose and out through your mouth using your belly as a barometer, notice the inflating with air and deflating. You do not have to change anything in your breathing, just notice it.

3. Remember, throughout this activity distraction will occur (external noises, random thoughts, etc.) and this is ok. Acknowledge they exist, yet allow them to flow and return to your breathing.

Let's Begin

Begin by bringing your attention to your body, as your either seated or laying down. You might want to close your eyes or keep them open. Do whatever is most comfortable for you.

Notice your bodies weight against the (chair, bed, couch)

As you take a deep breath in, and deep breath out. Notice any uncomfortable sensations and breathe them out. Visualize them leaving your body, soaring above you like a balloon flying away.

Now pay attention to your toes. You might want to wiggle them or just notice their presence. Are they tense or is there no feelings at all? Just take note. Imagine sending your breath all the way down to your toes as you take a deep breath in. As you exhale, imagine your breath traveling all the way up from your toes through your mouth. As you exhale, release the tension if it was there and if there wasn't any tension, it is ok.

When you are ready, let your toes dissolve out of your mind's eye and focus on your feet. As you bring your attention to your feet. Pay attention. 'Are they warm, are they cold, are they itchy or clammy" As you zoom in, you may begin to imagine your breath going to your feet, cooling it down if it is too hot, warming it up if it is too cold, easing the sensation of itching or drying the moistness. Choose whatever may be right for you in this moment.

Take a deep breath in and out

Shift your attention to your ankles, knees, and calves, as you continue to breathe in and out. Pay attention to the sensation or lack of sensation you may feel. Just notice, without taking any other action. As you breathe in and out, imagine for a moment your breath is traveling from your ankles, knees, and calves. As you exhale out, exhale any negative sensation you may have been feeling in your ankles, knees, and calves. As you exhale out, exhale any negative sensation you may have been feeling in your ankles, knees, and calves.

Take another deep breath in.

On your breath out shift your focus to the center of your body. Your torso, lower back, and hips. As you breathe, notice any tension, notice any pain, or discomfort you may feel. Notice your torso rising. As you breathe in, imagine the breaking up of all the tension, pain, or discomfort you may feel. Now take a long exhale releasing any the tension, releasing the pain, releasing the discomfort. Again, notice your torso begin to flatten, as the air is released and all the tension, pain and discomfort dissipates.

Take another deep breath in, and deep breath out.

Bring your attention now to your fingers. You may want to wiggle them, or just notice their presence. Are they tense, or is there any feeling at all? Just take note. Imagine for a moment, sending your breath as you inhale in, to the tip of each of your fingers. As you exhale, bring that same breath releasing any tension, traveling from the tips of your finger, through your arms, and neck and out through your mouth.

On your next inhale, begin to shift your awareness to your wrist, elbows, and arms. As you notice any sensation you may be feeling, you may want to pay attention to the difference your right arm, may feel from your left or there may be no difference at all. Just notice. As you begin to exhale, you may begin to feel your arms begin to soften, your wrist and elbows begin to be less rigid.

On your breath out, start to focus on your shoulders, neck, and upper back. You may begin to roll your shoulders, forward and back with each inhale and exhale. Now roll your neck in a circular motion as you pay attention to any stress you may be holding in this part of your body. Releasing it with every exhale out. Deep breath in, and deep breath out. Now direct your attention to your face, your head, and your scalp. Imagine as you inhale in, your breath rising from your torso to your face, through all the neurons in your brain, and out of your mouth.

Let your attention expand to your whole body. Feel the rhythm of your breath from the tips of your toes to the top of your head. Feel the rise and fall of your torso, as you inhale in and exhale out. Feel the delight in your body as you breathe out all the tension.

Take a deeper inhale in… hold it for a few seconds longer, and exhale out, as you imagine your breath floating away like a balloon.

Now start to bring your awareness back to the present. Back to where you are sitting or lying down. Back to this moment. Back to being fully alert.

You may open your eyes, whenever you are ready. Do what is comfortable for you. Now as you move forward to live in this moment, just remember the feeling you had, as you paid attention to your body and your breath and you attuned to yourself.

Praise yourself in this moment, for zooming into YOU!!!

THOUGHT SCAN: Zooming into your thoughts. (This works best when you practice daily or several times a day).

Let's Begin

You are going to take a moment to focus on your thoughts. Not the things you say out loud, but the ones you tell yourself. The thoughts you would never share, not even a best friend or close loved one. Focus on the thoughts which you say to yourself. The ones that you wish were not true. But question yourself, are they? Was there a time when your actions or vision of yourself was not aligned with the one you quietly tell yourself you are? Is there evidence that its true? Or is it a circumstance of the things you went through, the things you are not able to unsee. What if who you are, is the one other people see. The one that others love about you, the one that others admire about you, the ones that maybe hard for you to see. What if that was truly YOU? We talk to ourselves till it hurts us. Next time that negative thought or thoughts come through, ask yourself where is the evidence?

Praise yourself in this moment, for zooming into YOUR THOUGHTS!!!!

HEALING IS….

REDEFINING PURPOSE

Often, our perspective of purpose is viewed incorrectly. It is often viewed as a singular path, such as pursuing our dream job or being the perfect wife/husband. The question is, should it be? Should our purpose be focused on one thing or becoming a one-dimensional person. Does this mean we can only be passionate about one thing? What if pursuing our purpose causes us discomfort or heartache, does this mean it can no longer be our purpose? While we will remember, what we dreamt our purpose to be, we can turn our purpose into everyday living and strive to live for it all. It is not saying do not dream, its saying dream and remember to feel the sun shining, every day on your face. Remember the kind words someone spoke about you or you spoke to someone else. Purpose is LIVING. A quote that helps you redefine your purpose is, one from a movie.

The movie Hitch 2005 "life is not the amount of breaths you take. It's the moments that take your breath away". We would add, every moment should take our breath away because they all give our life meaning, not just one moment, one passion, one vision, one experience… they all do.

NOTICING:

What did you notice today?

Perhaps think of a previous moment in your day/week/ month. What did you see? If you were outside, did you see an array of people walking by or just a friendly face? Did you see the leaves floating by you, as they dance in the wind? Did you notice a squirrel speedily run through the street? Did you notice anything at all?

In your home, did you hear the buzzing of the walls when you were quiet or see the weird grain in the paint? Did you smell your favorite scent of lavender? Did you speak kind words to someone who needed it and you didn't even know, or are you still dreaming of the thing you have always wanted to do or be? Did you notice you, being you, and you are loved for it all? Even if you are not what you wanted to do or be.

NOTICING:

As you go through your day just notice it all

I will notice today

_____

_____

_____

I have noticed today

_____

_____

_____

The moment I wish I paid close attention to yesterday

_____

_____

_____

NOTICING:

As you go through your day just notice it

I will today

_____

_____

_____

I have noticed today

_____

_____

_____

The moment I wish I paid close attention to yesterday

_____

_____

_____

HEALING IS….

DIVINE CONNECTION

When you read divine connection, you may have assumed that we meant connection to a supreme being. It has nothing to do with an entity, it is coming into alignment, with yourself. When that happens, something magical begins to unfold. When your mind, body and soul become one, this is called self-alignment. By achieving self-alignment, you will get access to the divine presence all around us. Even when disappointments occur, you will still feel a sense of peace and contentment. If you allow this connection to bloom, you will feel joy, gratitude, and love, like you never imagined. That is "DIVINE CONNECTION".

Connecting to yourself:

FAVORITE PLACE TRANCE

Make yourself comfortable wherever you are. You may start by closing your eyes or finding a spot on the floor, as you take deep and long breaths, in and out. Concentrate on either your breathing or the spot on the floor and let your body become more relaxed and comfortable. Whenever you are ready, but soon, your eyes will be relaxed and comfortable that they may want to close, or that spot on the floor will be taking you in, as you become more relaxed and more comfortable. Continue to focus on your breathing. If your attention shifts, you may want to return to focusing on your breathing. As you get more relaxed and comfortable. You may begin to imagine for a moment, the favorite place you go. Where you feel at one with it all, including yourself. Is it the elliptical at the gym, or kayaking down the Delaware river, or staring at the sun as you feel its warmth on your skin? Wherever your place may be, imagine yourself there.

You may begin to smell your favorite smell, just as you like it. All the notes and undertones you remember from that place. You may begin to imagine the sounds you hear, as your favorite place becomes more in focus. Do you feel the feeling you feel, in that favorite space or place? The beat of your heart, the way it feels on your feet. You may be there by yourself, or maybe with someone special, enjoy your favorite place and person. As you smell, hear, feel that favorite place, it becomes more vivid. I can imagine you feel good in this place. You can do all the things you like to do there, when you are (what are you trying to reinvision for yourself… be connected to).

Stay as long as you would like. When you are almost ready to return, you will feel refreshed and relaxed.You will know what you need to do when you let yourself gradually return. Whenever you are ready. I would like you to come back to the present, where you are now. You can return to this favorite place whenever you would like.

HEALING IS....

PERSONAL CONNECTION

Resilience is an individual's capacity to adjust to, or recover from adversity, crisis, or difficulties that they may experience. It is vital to how we heal. Often, people believe that we have an innate ability to be resilient, but the truth is, nothing happens in a vacuum. In countless studies conducted regarding trauma, one of the primary factors that support healing and positive outcomes for those impacted by trauma is having responsive and positive relationships with others, a personal connection. It is the ability to communicate (both verbally and nonverbally), the ability to express our inner experience, share them with others, as well as recognize and empathize with the feelings in others. Be Curious!

Curiosity about self

How am I feeling emotionally

_____

_____

_____

How am I feeling physically

_____

_____

_____

Sometimes we do not recognize or pay attention to the fact that our emotions are often experienced through bodily sensations. It is important to not only identify how we are feeling, but where we are feeling it as well, so that we can share those with others. In the next page, identify various emotions that you may experience and the location in your body you experience those feelings. Utilize a different color for each emotion.

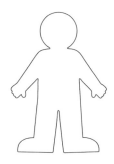

Legacy

Emotion

_____

Emotion

_____

Emotion

_____

Emotion

_____

Color

_____

Color

_____

Color

_____

Color

_____

Curiosity about others

Rate yourself on the quality of your relationships.

1. I check in with the people in my life?

←——————————————————————————————→

| Poor | Fair | Good | Excellent |

2. When I ask how they are doing, I listen to the answer?

←——————————————————————————————→

| Poor | Fair | Good | Excellent |

3. I have people in my life that I am able to share my feelings with?

←——————————————————————————————→

| Poor | Fair | Good | Excellent |

4. There are people in my life that I can ask for practical help (need someone to bring you to the doctor etc)?

←——————————————————————————————→

| Poor | Fair | Good | Excellent |

5. There are people in my life "who" can ask me for practical help (need someone to bring them to the doctor etc)?

←——————————————————————————————→

| Poor | Fair | Good | Excellent |

Looking at the way in which you rated your relationships, did you rate any poor or fair?

_____

- -

Were there any specific people you thought of during your rating?

_____

- -

If things were rated poorly, how can you improve?

_____

- -

_____

HEALING IS....

FINDING YOUR SPARK

It is simple really, it is about the thing that lights you up. This aligns with redefining your purpose, but its more. Its more than what you look for; it is how you live, how you connect and discover what makes you unique. It is difficult to do one without the other, because then you are lost. Create meaning making in your life.

MEANING MAKING

What inspires me: people, places and/or things?

_____

_____

What is the thing that makes me, who I am?

_____

_____

Where do I go when I get lost in my thoughts?

_____

_____

What do I enjoy doing for others?

_____

_____

HEALING IS....

LAUGHTER

Laugher is vital, and that is according to the science. According to article by the Mayo Clinic. Laughter does three things,

1. Stimulate organs, and allowing you to breathe in oxygen, whic increases the release of endorphins in the brain (pain and pleasure receptors)

2. Relieves the stress response by suppressing the stress hormone cortisol which is released during stressful times. The stress response is to fight, flight or freeze, in a dangerous situation to protect yourself. Danger does not have to be a lion chasing you, it can be worrying about how you are going to pay the bills tomorrow, it is many things. Chronic stress can lead to many chronic conditions.

3. Soothes tension by stimulating circulation and muscle relaxation.

<u>All these things are important while you discover the reinvisioned you</u>

JUST LAUGH

- It sounds easy, but do you remember the last time you laughed today? We will help.
- Think of a favorite scene from a movie, remember the first time you watched it. Laugh as if this was your first time.

- A memory that always makes you laugh, the time when you laughed at yourself or with someone else. Think of it again, as if it were happening right now.

- Just laugh for no reason, the one, the one that comes from the deepest part of your belly, the one that makes you laugh so hard you start crying.

Sometimes we have been through so many things that laughing is a luxury. With all the health benefits, it's not a luxury. It is necessity for a REINVISIONED YOU!!

HEALING IS....

DOING THE BRAVE

When people often think about vulnerability, it is often negative. It is often the thing we do not want to do, the thing that scares us the most. To be vulnerable is often synonymous with being weak. But as one of our favorite therapists, Brene Brown says, "being vulnerable is the most courageous thing we all can do". There is no weakness involved, just strength. It is opening yourself up and being seen and being heard, with no assurances that things are going to work out in your favor. If you are able to do that, do the brave and be vulnerable, you open up yourself to the possibility for something wonderful.

DARE AND JUST DO IT

Brene Brown wrote "daring greatly means the courage to be vulnerable. It means show up and be seen, to ask for what you need, to talk about how you are feeling and to have the hard conversation". It's the way to stay connected. Human connection is the necessary for our existence…

How was I vulnerable recently?

_____

_____

_____

_____

_____

FINDING WHO TO BE VULNERABLE WITH,

WHO IS YOUR TRIBE?

Your tribe is the people you feel safe with. People in your life reside in tiers like a cake. Some are on the top layer, the closest to you, and as the tiers expand, not that you cannot trust them. You may not open as much. Just because they are on the last tier, they are not glued there so things may change. Place who is your 3 layer tribe on the next page.

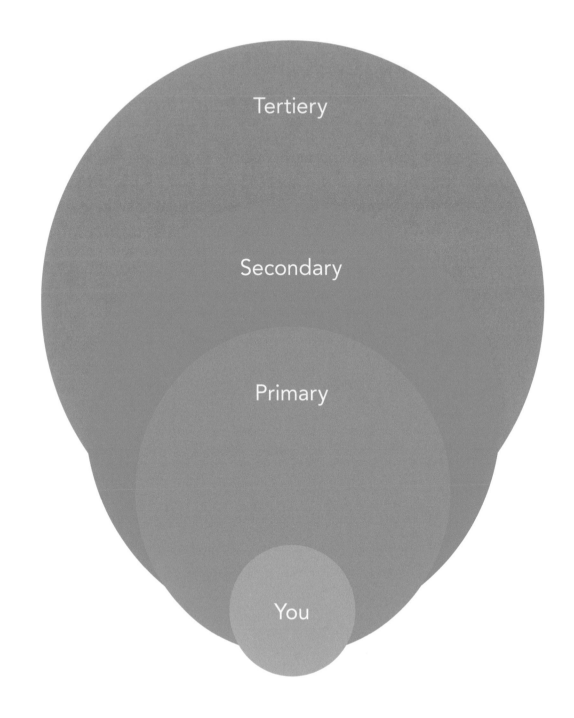

APPENDIX:

GRATITUDE CALANDER.
21 DAYS OF RADICAL GRATITUDE

Sun	Mon	Tue	Wed	Thu	Fri	Sat

Use the calendar above to challenge yourself to 21 days of finding moments
that you held on to, moment that you practiced radial gratitude.

30 DAY REFLECTION

MY FAVORITE MOMENTS

_____

_____

_____

_____

MY THOUGHTS

_____

_____

_____

_____

WHAT I HAVE LEARNED ABOUT MYSELF

_____

_____

_____

_____

POSITIVE AFFIRMATIONS

Our words are powerful, and the more you speak light into ourselves, the more that energy will exude, and greatness can happen.

EXAMPLE. I am more than enough.

I am doing the best I can, with what I have.

1. _____

2. _____

3. _____

4. _____

5. _____

6. _____

7. _____

8. _____

9. _____

10. _____

25 EASY SELF COMPASSION ACTIVITIES

1. Watch a funny video.
2. Put your phone away for 30 minutes.
3. Listen to relaxing music.
4. Say NO, to something you do not want to do.
5. Do 1 minute of deep breathing, inhale hold and exhale, each for a count of 7.
6. Place a post-it note on your mirror of a quote that inspires you, or one of your affirmations.
7. Sip on a cup of herbal tea and remember to smell the aroma with every sip.
8. Stretch.
9. Take a relaxing bath, do not forget the bubbles.
10. Buy yourself flowers.
11. Light your favorite candle.
12. Listen to an inspiring or fun podcast.
13. Cook your favorite meal.
14. Have dessert, in the middle of the day.
15. Color in an adult coloring book.
16. Go for a walk outside.
17. Pray or meditate.
18. Order food from your favorite restaurant.
19. Have a 5-minute dance session, to your favorite song.
20. Plant something.
21. Give yourself a manicure.
22. Send words of kindness to a friend, that you may not speak to often.
23. Pamper yourself, with what you like to do.
24. Practice RADICAL GRATITUDE.
25. DO SOMETHING YOU LOVE.

REFERENCES

Blaustein, M. & Kinniburgh, K. (2010). Treating traumatic stress in children and adolescents: How to foster resilience through attachment, self-regulation, and competency. New York: Guilford Press.

Brown, Brene (2012). *The Power of Vulnerability: Teaching on Authenticity, Connection, & Courage.* Sounds True.

Centers for Disease Control and Prevention. "Preventing Adverse Childhood Experiences." Retrieved from https://www.cdc.gov/violenceprevention/aces/fastfact.htm

Center on the Developing Child at Harvard University. "Toxic Stress." Retrieved from https://developingchild.harvard.edu/science/key-concepts/toxic-stress/

Tennant, A. (2005). Hitch. Columbia Pictures.

Printed in the United States
by Baker & Taylor Publisher Services